TURNING ASIDE TO HEAR
Word into Mid-Life Heart and Beyond

*Interactive Scripture-based meditations with relaxation
techniques for personal sacred-time or group use*

Anne Alcock

VERITAS

First published 2004 by
Veritas Publications
7/8 Lower Abbey Street
Dublin 1
Ireland
Email publications@veritas.ie
Website www.veritas.ie

ISBN 1 85390 877 0

10 9 8 7 6 5 4 3 2 1

A catalogue record for this book is available from the British Library.

Scripture quotations are taken from the *New Revised Standard Version
Bible* © 1993 and 1998 by the Division of Christian Education of the
National Council of the Churches of Christ in the USA; *The Living
Bible*, Tyndale House Publishers, 1976; *The New American Bible*, World
Bible Publishing, 1990; *The New Jerusalem Bible*, Darton, Longman and
Todd Ltd, 1990.

Cover design by Niamh McGarry
Printed in the Republic of Ireland by Betaprint Ltd., Dublin

*Veritas books are printed on paper made from the wood pulp of managed
forests. For every tree felled, at least one tree is planted, thereby renewing
natural resources.*

Christmas 2007

My Wish for you Chris!

Cecilia

The Lord bless you, and keep you;
The Lord's face shine on you,
And be gracious to you;
The Lord's countenance be lifted up to you,
And give you peace.

Num 6:24-26.

To my mother, Helena Alcock

CONTENTS

OPENING THE
FIRST PAGES

Why pick up this book? The cover? A word or phrase that speaks to you of your wish for quiet reflection? Whatever the reason, you may have noticed the 'interactive' at the beginning of the subtitle, telling you that this offers a body-mind-spirit approach and more than a passive read-through. You will also notice that the short relaxation before each Scripture passage are more sketched than etched. That is, they float questions rather than present answers, and there are pauses (indicated by a line of dots) for that prayerful interaction that is at the heart of any engagement with Scripture, and the Mystery which we call God. In other words, a scene is being set, for the heart and the Spirit. What may follow from that, as you move beyond the sketch into your own story, will hopefully bring a deepening spiritual connection to whatever aspect of life you are bringing here today, and further insight for the rest of your life.

Most of us have seen that familiar poster *Today is the First Day of the Rest of your Life* so often that for years we've passed it by without a second glance. Me too. Just recently, though, I've begun to realise that the 'rest of my life' is not simply an option in next season's holiday brochure, but is already here! This means I *am* giving a second glance. A second-half-of-*life* glance, if you like, as the number of days ahead are realistically fewer than those left behind.

Therefore 'today' and 'now' are important words! I want to cherish them by living them – here and now. Yet I often find I am running several parallel lives in my head, even though I claim to be living for the present moment. So I ask myself, 'Can I really live reflectively in the present moment, really experience, really feel, really taste, really pause?' Even with the misses and messes, contradictions, ambivalences and unfinished bits of today? Can I then rest with the fact that everything else (desk-diaries planning for two years hence, notwithstanding) waits in the queue for another day? For me, that ubiquitous poster challenges, kindly, and with concern, 'So how are you living today?' And I'd like my own heart's truthful answer to be, 'With appreciation'.

Perhaps you also find yourself wanting to savour both the innocence of childhood and the deeper insight of what really matters to us today. Perhaps you are experiencing a movement within yourself, from all-outward physical energy to more interior spiritual-energy. This of course happens naturally towards mid-life, the stage of life at which we ask questions about meaning, but may occur earlier due to the stress and responsibility that are part and parcel of modern living. As if we need to remember and discover the balance of some reflective, renewing, quiet-time every day, as a soul-need, rather than, as Wayne Muller puts it, 'a lifestyle suggestion'.[1]

Reflective time allows for the sort of evaluation that recognises this life of mine as unique, precious, and my own responsibility despite whatever roles and dependencies have been part of it up to now, and in spite of those that will come in the future. We should view our life as a substantial gift, surely worth taking time to unpack beyond the first layer. Our choice to take time allows also for a gathering of all that has been so far, and perhaps a new inclusivity: 'Yes, I do accept this now', 'I hadn't thought of doing that before'. It lets me move gently with that distinctive shift in values, from what are called ego-concerns, to what seem more soul-concerns. These include quality of life, for yourself, for others, for the Earth, a desire to be more Creation-connected, and more centred in stillness. And somewhere in this mid-life movement, whatever age or stage it hits us, thirty-five, forty-five, fifty, or on the threshold of retirement, we may find our priorities changing. As a new light shines on areas formerly in shadow we may realise that living with honesty, integrity and generosity matter more than material gain. A door opens to the wisdom dimension, and our gaze becomes an overview. As one later-mid-life friend reflected, 'I feel my life as a three-phase journey; conquering the world, enjoying the world and returning the world to the Maker, through gratitude.'

All the reflections in this book are intended to honour the second two phases of that journey. Having conquered, tried to, or discovered we really never do, perhaps it is time to enjoy the present moment. This book is intended for personal prayer-space, and some of the reflections would also suit a group setting, especially those with a specific visualisation. The themes come from those aspects of mid-life experience that the chosen Scripture passages seem to illuminate. However, they will undoubtedly lead you further and deeper, and depending on where and how you happen to pause and find yourself today, in your own circumstances of body, mind and spirit. And because feelings and situations change, the chapters are presented in no particular order. Rather, taking example from the Psalter where moments of peace follow close on the heels of frustration and transition the only structure will be your own.[2]

Most of the passages chosen could probably gather under the heading 'Old Favourites' – Scripture passages reflecting and enduring the expansions and contractions of life. As it happens, several involve the appearance of an angel and although the inclusion of so many wasn't intentional, perhaps it is timely, since angels are featuring more and more in recent publications. Of course they were always there, out of sight for a while, but never really out of mind. All the passages, with or without angels, have been used for many years as texts for individual and group retreats, guided prayer-days and in personal time, and one way offered towards 'disposing the heart' for the Word, has been through the use of relaxation and breathing exercises. Relaxation places us where we are, right here. (The word 'disposing' comes from the Latin *'ponere'*, 'to place'!) Hence the inclusion of the short breathing exercises mentioned above. You will find two alternating breath sequences for calming, at the beginning of each chapter, and then you have the full muscle relaxation and/or hand massage following this introduction, before the Scripture and the guided reflection.

After that it's over to you and the Mystery which is spiritual relationship...

DEEP RELAXATION SKILLS

Each scripture passage is accompanied by one of two short breathing relaxation skills within individual chapters. For those readers who have time for or require a more sustained exercise, the hand and/or muscle relaxation skills beneath should be used as a replacement.

[READ SCRIPTURE PASSAGE]

SKILL 1: HAND RELAXATION

You might like to start off by quietening with a short, easy hand-relaxation.

This simple sequence soon becomes automatic, and only takes about seven minutes on each hand.

Sitting comfortably and consciously relaxing your shoulders by lifting, briefly holding, and then lowering your shoulders, place your right thumb into the centre of your left palm.

Now just roll and press the right thumb pad around that left palm. Keep the shoulders soft and low.

Relax your jaw by slightly opening your back teeth.

Now let your right thumb find the centre of the receiving palm: press, and breathe deeply in and out a couple of times, slowly, as though sighing.

Now let your thumb walk upwards on that palm, bending like a little caterpillar up the little spaces between the lower bases of second, third, fourth and fifth fingers.

Then use the thumb and fingers of your giving hand to roll and press that fleshy 'V' of skin joining the base of the receiving thumb to the rest of the hand. From there, move up to the pad of the receiving thumb and press all round both pad and tip with the giving thumb, and then with the second finger of that giving hand, press all round the edge of the nail.

Finally, gently massage each finger from base to nail, and finish with an all over palm and back of hand rub.

Another relaxing outbreath and shoulder-check, and you're ready to repeat this with the other hand.

So, this time, place your left thumb into the centre of your right palm.

Now just roll and press the left thumb pad around the right palm. Keep the shoulders soft and low.

Relax your jaw. Now let that giving thumb find the centre of the receiving palm; press, and breathe deeply in and out a couple of times, as though sighing.

Now let your thumb walk upwards from that centre palm, up between the bases of the second and third, third and fourth and fourth and fifth finger bones.

Again use the thumb and fingers of your giving hand to roll and press that 'V' of skin joining the base of the receiving thumb to the rest of the hand.

From there, move up to the pad of the receiving thumb and press all round both tip and pad, and then with the second finger of the giving hand, press round the edge of the nail.

Finally, gently massage each finger from base to nail, and finish with an all over rub – palm and back of hand – on both hands, then leave them resting comfortably in your lap, or cupped in receiving posture.

Now slowly re-read the Scripture passage, line by line, pausing inwardly, listening, and considering any part of your life to which these words might especially be speaking ...

[READ REFLECTION]
[END RELAXATION TECHNIQUE]

[READ SCRIPTURE PASSAGE]

SKILL 2: MUSCLE RELAXATION

You can begin, if you wish, with some progressive muscle relaxation, before moving into the meditation.

Begin by becoming aware of the points of contact between your body and the chair (or your body and the floor). Become aware of the chair or floor beneath you, and allow it to support your body.

Relax any tightness of your tummy muscles with a slow out-breath... warm air breathed out, cool air breathed in and felt on your upper lip.

Now imagining yourself floating into warm darkness for a moment, allow your eyes to close. Bring your attention down to your right foot... Without moving the whole leg, gently point the toes, move the ankle gently up and down once or twice... then rest it again.

Now tighten the muscles of your right leg probably most obviously above the knee. Hold the tension a moment or two, and then release it, feeling that right leg relaxed and softly heavy.

Turn your attention now to your left foot. Again, point the toes, gently move the ankle up and down once or twice, and then rest it. Tighten the muscles of your left leg, hold the tension a moment or two, and then release it.

Feel the soft heaviness in both legs and feet, and move them if they need a different position for complete relaxation. Now, on an out-breath, relax the muscles around your waist and let yourself sigh.

Then relax your shoulders by lifting and lowering them two or three times, feeling the stretch, towards your ears (if lying down, let them sink downwards and slightly backwards).

Make a fist with your right hand, then a star with open fingers, and then a fist again, this time tightening the arm, locking the elbow, and feel the stretch from your wrist, through the forearm, upper arm to your neck muscles. Breathe in once, hold it a moment, and then exhale and relax the whole arm and hand.

Now make a fist with your left hand, then a star with open fingers, and then again a fist, this time tightening the arm, locking the elbow, and feeling the stretch, again feeling the tightness in your forearm, upper arm and neck muscles. Breathe in once, hold it a moment and then release breath and arm tension. Relax.

Move your head and neck slowly from side to side, and with a very gentle forward nod, find the most comfortable position...

Now become aware of your own ordinary breathing rhythm. Don't force it or try and change it, just become aware of it.

Cool air breathed in, warm air breathed out... gently... evenly... as you enter into the reflection... and now, taking a deep breath, gently begin to move fingers... and toes...

Gently move yours shoulders around, and move your head from side to side.

Take another deep breath, exhale, and just relax until you are ready to move on from this space.

[READ REFLECTION]
[END RELAXATION TECHNIQUE]

A NOTE BEFORE BEGINNING

After each Scripture passage the reader will find a series of dots reappearing again and again within each reflection. The function of these dots or ellipses is to encourage the reader to pause, visualise and reflect on what has come before, considering the significance of the given image or sketch to one's own life. This pausing is essential to the interactive structure of the book and readers are urged to utilise this opportunity for meaningful meditation before continuing on with the reflection.

Chapter I

DON'T BE AFRAID

But now the Lord who created you, O Israel,
says,
Don't be afraid,
for I have ransomed you;
I have called you by name;
you are mine.
When you go through deep waters and great trouble,
I will be with you.
When you go through rivers of difficulty,
you will not drown!
When you walk through the fire of oppression
You will not be burned up –
The flames will not consume you...
For I am the Lord your God, your Saviour...
... you are precious to me and honoured, and I love
you.
Don't be afraid, for I am with you.'

Isa 43:1-3a, 4b-5a LB

SHORT BREATHING RELAXATION SKILL 1

Before beginning the meditation, you may like to relax with a couple of simple shoulder and tummy breaths.

So first, just raise your shoulders towards your jaw, and hold them there for a moment, and then let them down again. Now repeat once more, only this time consciously, but naturally breathe in as you lift your shoulders, holding the breath a moment and then exhaling easily like a sigh, as you let your shoulders drop. Repeat one more time, and let yourself become aware of where and how you are, as you come to this reflection.

Re-read the Scripture text, and perhaps take a listening moment with it in quietness before turning to the reflective meditation.

I wonder
what I am *really* called...?

**I have called you by name;
you are mine...**

I reflect on the many names I hear
which refer to me...
Names that are titles...
Roles...
Job-descriptions...

The name that links me to
an organisation or an institution or a family...
Ex-names
and nicknames, pet names ... what else?...
I reflect on this...
Who am I?...

For after all those,
I ask, 'is there another '*me*'

an '*I am*'
that You know
that I know?'...

A name
that
despite puzzles,
despite struggles,
I recognise...
And yes, actually love –
if I can admit that.
Is this the name
with
its flickering, sometimes glowing tones
of unique colour
which
I first heard whispered
at my conception?...

The name continuously given
towards my Completion.
I pray with this...

**When you go through deep waters and great trouble,
I will be with you...**

I read my name at the end of this sentence
and I am reassured.
'Deep water, great trouble –'
You never said these wouldn't be there
singly; together.

But you say that you are here within it...
Somehow?
To see us through...

See *me* through?
So where are you, God, in *this*?...
I pray...

Dare I take a breath now?
And another...
And...
In my imagination,
I place myself a little distance
above any situation I experience as deep water or trouble
and I name it...
So...
I create a little zone of safety.
And I notice how it feels to look down, even in imagination,
from a chosen separated space...

When you go through rivers of difficulty, you will not drown!...

In the midst of the tumult, I hear the word 'through'
You are telling me I will go through,
and get through?...

And 'through' means 'I'll come out'.
'Yes. There was a beginning
I have lived through difficulty before, I will live again.
There will be an ending.'

Then –
a new beginning
a further start...
Through it all

So I pray
let the waters surge me onwards
trusting, believing
those words,
you will not drown...

While
carefully,
deliberately,
gratefully,
I hand it over.

Praying through this...

Now take a moment or two to gather any insight or word you would want to take away from this time. Sense how you are feeling, body, mind and spirit, and sense how you go on from here into today or tonight... Go well.

Chapter 2

WHERE HAVE I COME FROM, WHERE AM I GOING?

The Angel of the Lord found her beside a desert spring along the road to Shur.
The Angel: 'Hagar, Sarai's maid, where have you come from and where are you going?'
Hagar: 'I am running away from my mistress.'
The Angel: 'Return to your mistress and act as you should, for I will make you into a great nation.'

GEN 16:7-9 LB

SHORT BREATHING RELAXATION SKILL 2

Before beginning the meditation here is a second deep breath exercise you may wish to try. Lifting your shoulders, bring them inward and upward towards your ears, and hold them there for a moment, aware of the stretch and the warmth that goes with it, as you let the shoulders back down. Repeat this a second and third time, and then, bending your elbows, move your shoulder blades together, and gently 'wing' your elbows in and out, together and then separately, to soften and relax the muscles of your back. Now return your arms and hands to your lap, and just breathe out as though sighing. Now, for a count of four, inhale through your nose, aware of how your lower ribcage expands outwards, and then the mid-chest, and upper chest. Give a

*final little 'sniff' inwards before gently exhaling again through your
mouth for a count of six, (or eight if you can do so easily). Don't force
anything. Repeat this whole deep breath just once more, and then
resume your ordinary breathing.*

*Now slowly read the Scripture text again and see where it takes
you....*

Hagar...
Cautious...
Escaping...

Hagar
with ambivalent loyalties,
And nowhere to go.

She's running now,
anything to keep moving
to get beyond the feelings
'Taken for granted'...
'Used'...
'Confused'...
'Let down'...

Tiring,

she reaches the well.

You see her
and stand with her,
both together at the well...
A well of wisdom and comfort
for this time of running

Standing there,
you confirm for yourself,
what makes it a well,
a resource?

Is it a place?

A person?

An insight?

Something else?
You reflect on this…

And then
with Hagar,
you turn to the Angel of this well
who asks the question first, of Hagar;
'Where have you come from, Where are you going?'
You hear Hagar's reply,
'I am running away'…

Now the question
is for you,
'Where have you come from, Where are you going?'
You ask yourself,
'Where have I come from?'…
'Where am I going?'…

The angel has said to Hagar
'return'
and you wonder –
your situation is different,
but you find yourself asking the angel
*'What needs to be done
Before I run really free?'*…
Reflecting, 'What truth will set me free?…
What word?…
What action?'…

You know
it is right.
And a strength has come at this well,
calmer, stronger, reoriented...
You stay with Hagar
and what this Messenger still has to say...

And pray from this...

Now take a moment or two to gather any insight or word you would want to take away from this time. Sense how you are feeling, body, mind and spirit, and sense how you go on from here into today or tonight... Go well.

Chapter 3

TRANSITIONS

'For I know the plans I have for you,' says the Lord
'they are plans for good
and not for evil
to give you a future
and a hope.
In the days when you pray,
I will listen.
You will find me when you seek me
if you look for me in earnest.'

JER 29:11-13 LB

SHORT BREATHING RELAXATION SKILL 1

Before beginning the meditation, you may like to relax with a couple of simple shoulder and tummy breaths.

So first, just raise your shoulders towards your jaw, and hold them there for a moment, and then let them down again. Now repeat once more, only this time consciously, but naturally breathe in as you lift your shoulders, holding the breath a moment and then exhaling easily like a sigh, as you let your shoulders drop. Repeat one more time, and let yourself become aware of where and how you are, as you come to this reflection.

Re-read the Scripture text, and perhaps take a listening moment with it in quietness before turning to the reflective meditation.

For I know the plans I have for you, says the Lord...

A relief.
At last someone who knows,
even as I admit
that right now,
I feel I don't...

Because
transition feels like 'All change'–
A different landscape from the same window...

Plans – wide plans, broad-sweep plans
Your Plans...
If only they could silence
the chattering
of the different planners in my head.
Plan A and B and C
or none of them.
It's still rather soon.

When all I know is
disconnection...

A plug has been pulled
and I have been switched off
from
much of what I feel connected with before.

(Help me connect with your plan...)

And then, in this in-between time,
I find I wonder, 'who *am* I now?'...
As if I might no longer be who I was
known roles disappearing...

And a stranger peering back at me
from the mirror.

(Help me know who I am in your plan...)

Yet – within
unsureness holds itself
the seeds of re-creation,
reorientation.

My steps turning differently
from disorientation through to re-orientation.
Help me find direction in your plan...

And now, once more, I read your words
very slowly.

I set my name after each full stop.
Giving me pause from running ahead
of your spirit.

This is how transition is.
This mid-way experience
its own cycle, repeated,
from Goodbye to Hello,
this special time
called 'Waiting'
which is now...

**they are plans for good
and not for evil....**

Heightened awareness
unfamiliarity, yes
but collaborating heart
with what will be good;
'made, loved, sustained'.
This doesn't change.

Expectations
and
future
held more loosely
treading tenderly, justly,
respectful of dreams.
Each breath tells me
Change is inevitable, growth is optional...

You offer me growth.
Even yet.

**In the days when you pray,
I will listen...
You will find me when you seek me
if you look for me in earnest...**

Prayer from the heart
and each event bringing me
guidance.
I recognise what I can't always name –
Your presence...
Your plans...
And
Plans having their starting point.
Right here.
With all I am and have.
I have choices...

*Now take a moment or two to gather any insight or word you would
want to take away from this time. Sense how you are feeling, body,
mind and spirit, and sense how you go on from here into today or
tonight... Go well.*

Chapter 4

HOLDING ONTO LIFE

(Hagar) went out into the wilderness ... wandering aimlessly. When the water was gone she left the child beneath a bush and went off and sat down a hundred yards or so away. 'I don't want to watch him die,' she said, and burst into tears, sobbing wildly.

Then God answered the lad's cries, and the Angel of God called to her from the sky, 'Hagar, what's wrong? Don't be afraid! For God has heard the lad's cries as he is lying there. Go and get the boy and comfort him, for I will make a great nation from his descendants.' Then God opened her eyes and she saw a well; so she refilled the container and gave the lad a drink.

GEN 21: 14-20 LB

SHORT BREATHING RELAXATION SKILL 2

Before beginning the meditation here is a second deep breath exercise you may wish to try. Lifting your shoulders, bring them inward and upward towards your ears, and hold them there for a moment, aware of the stretch and the warmth that goes with it, as you let the shoulders back down. Repeat this a second and third time, and then, bending your elbows, move your shoulder blades together, and gently 'wing' your elbows in and out, together and then separately, to soften and relax the muscles of your back. Now return your arms and hands to your lap, and just breathe out as though sighing. Now, for a count of four, inhale through your nose, aware of how your lower ribcage expands outwards, and then the mid-chest, and upper chest. Give a final little 'sniff' inwards before gently exhaling again through your mouth for a count of six, (or eight if you can do this easily). Don't force anything. Repeat this whole deep breath just once more, and then resume your ordinary breathing.

Now slowly read the Scripture text again and see where it takes you....

You take time to let the scene appear,
your senses creating
Colour...
Shape...
Sound...
Scent...
Or taste...
Visualising the wilderness expanse before you,
and then finding Hagar there,
Abraham's water-jar strapped to her shoulders,
walking as it says, 'aimlessly' just ahead...

And as you meet her here,
it is as if you are able to become her, enter her skin
able to find further words
that describe desert and the way of being in it...

The pace...
The reason...
The feeling...
At this time...
You pray with this...

You find yourself asking
what, if anything,
has been placed on your own shoulders
in the recent or more distant past,
and by whom? and why?
and why you carry it still...

You reflect on your own inner water supply...
The level
Going up...
Going down...
How you know when it needs replenishment,
and what that means,
praying with this...

And, now,
you become aware,
like Hagar,
that you carry something precious
the child of life.
Something which wants to reveal itself as
A gift...
A talent...
A dream...
A voice...

And you reflect on how this is being nourished,
could be nourished
by you...
By what circumstances...

You see how Hagar
places her child under a bush...
Half-hidden...
How she moves away – sits apart
and you reflect,
What of that precious life within me?...

What bush do I find that keeps it hidden,
out of sight...
almost out of my mind...

And yet claiming life
'I don't want to watch *what* die?'
You ask
Is there anything yet unlived that reaches out to life?...
Am I also 'sitting down' at a little distance?...
And how do I know this?...
You pray with this...

And now,
you hear the inner cry
words, tone
and what you longed for...

Until
together with that voice
you hear
the voice of the Angel...
The cry has been heard

Your eyes open too.
You can move,
You can see the well.
You can drink, and give to drink.
You pray with this...

Now take a moment or two to gather any insight or word you would want to take away from this time. Sense how you are feeling, body, mind and spirit, and sense how you go on from here into today or tonight... Go well.

Chapter 5

INTIMACY

*'But I will court her again, and bring her into the
wilderness, and speak to her tenderly there. There I
will give back her vineyards to her, and transform her
Valley of Troubles to a Door of Hope. She will
respond to me there, singing for joy as in days long
ago in her youth....'*

Hos 2:14-15 LB

SHORT BREATHING RELAXATION SKILL 1

*Before beginning the meditation, you may like to relax with a couple
of simple shoulder and tummy breaths.*

*So first, just raise your shoulders towards your jaw, and hold them
there for a moment, and then let them down again. Now repeat once
more, only this time consciously, but naturally breathe in as you lift
your shoulders, holding the breath a moment and then exhaling easily
like a sigh, as you let your shoulders drop. Repeat one more time, and
let yourself become aware of where and how you are, as you come to
this reflection.*

*Re-read the Scripture text, and perhaps take a listening moment
with it in quietness before turning to the reflective meditation.*

You remember a photograph –
the one taken of you
around First Communion…
With prayer books, white-covered,
little 'colour plates' on glossy paper,
or tissue thin with leather, and plaited ribbon binding
and the rosary
coloured or pearl or luminous
statues, high to reach and cool to touch…
The red flicker of the Lamp;
smaller lights, and holy pictures
that showed you Heaven…
Experiencing God.
Remember?
Pray with this…..

You remember a photograph –
a team, a class, a group…
School moments caught in a frame.
Fun, friends…
feelings…
fantasies…
Remember?
Pray with this…

You remember a photograph,
another group, but smaller
books and desks,
examination…
Wider thresholds, widening world…
Remember?
Pray with this…

You remember a photograph –
a young adult dreams…

Delights with discovery...
Colour prints...
Willing strengths...
God in this...

Spirituality defined,
responsible time –
decisions....
Commitments...
Fallings, failings...
Faith remember?
Pray with this...

You remember a photograph
capturing the realist
the worker
no illusions
no delusions.
The tyranny of the clock
and meetings –
meeting expectations
spirit struggle
suffocating under schedules...

Winding on –
no need for a photograph
you are already here,
and the invitation is becoming sweet again.
Smile –
as
space stretches more comfortably
to accommodate time
and I can say
not now, not yet or not ever...

Time with
God, my God,
Quieter now
more spacious now.
Invitation to stillness...
Invitation to Sabbath...

You are found
You have found
indwelling
the One you rest with
quietly familiar.
Relationship
is recognition...

Now take a moment or two to gather any insight or word you would want to take away from this time. Sense how you are feeling, body, mind and spirit, and sense how you go on from here into today or tonight... Go well.

Chapter 6

THE PSALM OF
THE HEART

O Lord, you have examined my heart
and know everything about me.
You know when I sit or stand.
When far away,
you know my every thought.
You chart the path ahead of me,
and tell me where to stop and rest.
Every moment you know where I am.
You know what I am going to say before I even say
it.
You both precede and follow me, and place your
hand of blessing on my head.

Ps 139:1-5 LB

SHORT BREATHING RELAXATION SKILL 2

Before beginning the meditation here is a second deep breath exercise
you may wish to try. Lifting your shoulders, bring them inward and
upward towards your ears, and hold them there for a moment, aware
of the stretch and the warmth that goes with it, as you let the
shoulders back down. Repeat this a second and third time, and then,
bending your elbows, move your shoulder blades together, and gently

'wing' your elbows in and out, together and then separately, to soften and relax the muscles of your back. Now return your arms and hands to your lap, and just breathe out as though sighing. Now, for a count of four, inhale through your nose, aware of how your lower ribcage expands outwards, and then the mid-chest, and upper chest. Give a final little 'sniff' inwards before gently exhaling again through your mouth for a count of six, (or eight if you can do this easily). Don't force anything. Repeat this whole deep breath just once more, and then resume your ordinary breathing.

Now slowly read the Scripture text again and see where it takes you....

O Lord, you know my heart...

I reflect on what is going on for me at this moment...
Not judging,
not changing
just truthfully,
simply,
aware...
What words I put on present feelings...
What feelings attach to this week's activities...
The activities that make up my life...
And what my life means to me today...

You know everything about me.
You know when I sit or stand.
When far away you know my every thought...

Sometimes it is easy to feel far away – want to be far away
sometimes I have no words,
but you Lord, know my thoughts...
My wanderings,
You understand...

You chart the path ahead of me,
and tell me where to stop and rest...

Lord, help me to listen to my body
to recognise the hints of when to
slow down...
Take rest...
And how...

Every moment you know where I am...

And when I feel lost,
remind me where to look
rediscover, rekindle,
reframe...

You know what I am going to say before I even say it.
You both precede and follow me, and place your hand of blessing
on my head...

Whether I have something to say, or just silence
allow that blessing in,
imagining light, or warmth or colour,
flowing through me, around me,
breathing in
until, in the still centre of it,
I meet the source.
I meet You...

Now take a moment or two to gather any insight or word you would
want to take away from this time. Sense how you are feeling, body,
mind and spirit, and sense how you go on from here into today or
tonight... Go well.

Chapter 7

TRULY SAFE

This is too glorious,
too wonderful to believe.
I can never be lost to your spirit.
I can never get away from my God.
If I go up to heaven you are there;
If I go down to the place of the dead, you are there.
If I ride the morning winds to the farthest oceans,
even there your hand will guide me, your strength
will support me.
If I try to hide in the darkness, the night becomes
light around me.
For even darkness cannot hide from God; to you the
night shines as bright as day. Darkness and light are
both alike to you.

Ps 139: 6-12 LB

SHORT BREATHING RELAXATION SKILL 1

Before beginning the meditation, you may like to relax with a couple of simple shoulder and tummy breaths.

So first, just raise your shoulders towards your jaw, and hold them there for a moment, and then let them down again. Now repeat once more, only this time consciously, but naturally breathe in as you lift your shoulders, holding the breath a moment and then exhaling easily like a sigh, as you let your shoulders drop. Repeat one more time, and let yourself become aware of where and how you are, as you come to this reflection.

Re-read the Scripture text, and perhaps take a listening moment with it in quietness before turning to the reflective meditation.

This is too glorious,
too wonderful to believe.
I can never be lost to your spirit...

A truth that makes me
laugh in confirmation.
Your spirit in me
and as long as I have breath,
and beyond,
You are there...

I can never get away from my God...

My Ground-of-Being, *my God*
What does this mean?...
Am I glad?...
Would I want escape
indwelling God?...
Sometimes
of course
and yet...

If I go up to heaven you are there;
if I go down to the place of the dead, you are there...

Mood or circumstance
do not determine your presence.
Whether life today is heaven
light with inward song
lifting
or
whether
shadows further darken
a deadness...
You are there...

If I ride the morning winds to the farthest oceans,
even there your hand will guide me, your strength will support
me...

And when I lie in bed and dream,
eager for what can now
be possibility.
It is you who invite me to adventure
supported...

If I try to hide in the darkness, the night becomes light around me.
For even darkness cannot hide from God; to you the night shines
as bright as day. Darkness and light are both alike to you...

I have the practice of the years.
Yes, I can pretend
and manipulate and hide,
but
ultimately,
no one is fooled...

No one is freed...
Let me dare truth...
My truth
without ambiguity...
Without ambivalence
It's time...

Now take a moment or two to gather any insight or word you would want to take away from this time. Sense how you are feeling, body, mind and spirit, and sense how you go on from here into today or tonight... Go well.

Chapter 8

BEFORE I WAS BORN...

You made all the delicate, inner parts of my body,
and knit them together in my mother's womb.
Thank you for making me so wonderfully complex!
It is amazing to think about.
Your workmanship is marvellous – and how well I
*   know it.*
You were there while I was being formed in utter
*   seclusion!*
You saw me before I was born
and scheduled each day of my life before I began to
*   breathe.*

Ps 139: 13-16A LB

SHORT BREATHING RELAXATION SKILL 2

Before beginning the meditation here is a second deep breath exercise you may wish to try. Lifting your shoulders, bring them inward and upward towards your ears, and hold them there for a moment, aware of the stretch and the warmth that goes with it, as you let the shoulders back down. Repeat this a second and third time, and then, bending your elbows, move your shoulder blades together, and gently 'wing' your elbows in and out, together and then separately, to soften and relax the muscles of your back. Now return your arms and hands to your lap, and just breathe out as though sighing. Now, for a count of four, inhale through your nose, aware of how your lower ribcage expands outwards, and then the mid-chest, and upper chest. Give a final little 'sniff' inwards before gently exhaling again through your mouth for a count of six, (or eight if you can do this easily). Don't force anything. Repeat this whole deep breath just once more, and then resume your ordinary breathing.

Now slowly read the Scripture text again and see where it takes you....

You made all the delicate, inner parts of my body, and knit them together in my mother's womb...

I look at my hands –
each one
distinctive.
Fingers, lines, nails –
such detail
such history.
Thank you...

My own body shape,
inherited, accepted, (or trying to)
and recognisably
connecting me with my relatives,

my family line...
Thank you...

Thank you for making me so wonderfully complex!
It is amazing to think about.
Your workmanship is marvellous – and how well I know it...

I observe and ponder
how skin heals
and renews itself,
how joints and tissue support my bones...

I breathe normally
in and out,
and I reflect on
the rhythms
of expansion
and contraction
of lungs co-operating with heart,
and on all the systems
working for wholeness...
Thank you...

I bring my attention
to any
illness
or injury
or healing process –
Mind, body or spirit...
And I thank you...
You attend on this too...

You were there while I was being formed in utter seclusion!
You saw me before I was born
and scheduled each day of my life before I began to breathe.

My birthday –
let us celebrate
the date and time and place...
The season, the hour –
my hour, my mother, your choice...
And I listen for your song of my birth...

Now take a moment or two to gather any insight or word you would want to take away from this time. Sense how you are feeling, body mind and spirit, and sense how you go on from here into today or tonight... Go well.

Chapter 9

THE POTTER'S HANDS

'Come, go down to the potter's house, and there I will let you hear my words. So I went down to the potter's house, and there he was working at his wheel. The vessel he was making of clay was spoiled in the potter's hand, and he reworked it into another vessel, as seemed good to him.

JER 18: 2-4 NRSV

SHORT BREATHING RELAXATION SKILL 1

Before beginning the meditation, you may like to relax with a couple of simple shoulder and tummy breaths.

So first, just raise your shoulders towards your jaw, and hold them there for a moment, and then let them down again. Now repeat once more, only this time consciously, but naturally breathe in as you lift your shoulders, holding the breath a moment and then exhaling easily like a sigh, as you let your shoulders drop. Repeat one more time, and let yourself become aware of where and how you are, as you come to this reflection.

Re-read the Scripture text, and perhaps take a listening moment with it in quietness before turning to the reflective meditation.

In your imagination,
taking your time
letting your senses
guide you to the Potter's house...

Letting the scene unfold –
colour and shape and size,
you see the walls and windows,
the tables, shelves,
and different clays safely protected from drying...
The water-bowls for soaking and restoring...
And the Potter at the wheel...
Stay with this...

And you watch the Potter
focused, absorbed
careful with preparation.
Unhurried, readying the wheel
for a palmed handful of clay...

Poised to set it at the centre,
equal space all round.
Stay with this...

A funnel of clay rises from the circle
seemingly steady, the inner fold widening.
And then suddenly,
a tear, a wobble and it has spun away from the centre
spattering...

As you stay with this...
It is almost as if you have become that clay.
Skidding sometimes towards outer spheres
slipping from the centre

fallen from support
lumpy and uneven...

And the potter?
Strong hands are gentle now,
working a different surface, off the wheel.
And the lump is smoothed, soothed
No rush...
no force...

And a new form emerges
stretched, re-shaped
from the marks of the spin.
New beauty...
Stay as this...

Now take a moment or two to gather any insight or word you would want to take away from this time. Sense how you are feeling, body mind and spirit, and sense how you go on from here into today or tonight... Go well.

Chapter 10

END OF TETHER

'I've had enough,' Elijah told the Lord. 'Take away my life. I've got to die sometime and it might as well be now'. Then he lay down and slept beneath the broom bush. But as he was sleeping, an angel touched him and told him to get up and eat. He looked around and saw some bread baking on hot stones, and a jar of water! So he ate and drank and lay down again. Then the angel of the Lord came again and touched him and said, 'Get up and eat some more, for there is a long journey ahead of you'. So he got up and ate and drank, and the food gave him enough strength to travel forty days and forty nights to Mount Horeb, the mountain of God, where he lived in a cave. But the Lord said to him, 'What are you doing here, Elijah?'

1 KINGS 19:4B-9 LB

Short Breathing Relaxation Skill 2

Before beginning the meditation here is a second deep breath exercise you may wish to try. Lifting your shoulders, bring them inward and upward towards your ears, and hold them there for a moment, aware of the stretch and the warmth that goes with it, as you let the shoulders back down. Repeat this a second and third time, and then, bending your elbows, move your shoulder blades together, and gently 'wing' your elbows in and out, together and then separately, to soften and relax the muscles of your back. Now return your arms and hands to your lap, and just breathe out as though sighing. Now, for a count of four, inhale through your nose, aware of how your lower ribcage expands outwards, and then the mid-chest, and upper chest. Give a final little 'sniff' inwards before gently exhaling again through your mouth for a count of six, (or eight if you can do this easily). Don't force anything. Repeat this whole deep breath just once more, and then resume your ordinary breathing.

Now slowly read the Scripture text again and see where it takes you...

It is hard to live
when you only live because you cannot die.
Or so it feels.
Elijah felt it, said it
to you
yet your angel was there
before he even woke.

So wake me
to the Angel's appearance in my life
today...
Just one appearance
is enough.

Wake me
to

remind me
of what
the Angel
has already provided for me...

Other times
when I was hungry...
Tired...
Defeated...
Lonely...
Frustrated...
Confused...
Just one reminder
Is enough...

Then I could ask that Angel
What am I being given
right here
this moment?...

Wake me...

Show me...

Now take a moment or two to gather any insight or word you would
want to take away from this time. Sense how you are feeling, body
mind and spirit, and sense how you go on from here into today or
tonight... Go well.

Chapter 11

WAITING IT OUT

*'Go out and stand before me on the mountain', the
Lord said to him.
And as Elijah stood there, the Lord passed by,
and a mighty windstorm hit the mountain;
it was such a terrible blast
 that the rocks were torn loose,
but the Lord was not in the wind.
After the wind,
there was an earthquake,
but the Lord was not in the earthquake.
And after the earthquake there was a fire,
but the Lord was not in the fire.
 And after the fire,
there was the sound of a gentle whisper.
When Elijah heard it, he wrapped his face in his
scarf and went out and stood at the entrance of the
cave.
And a voice said, 'Why are you here, Elijah?'*

1 KINGS 19: 11-13 LB

SHORT BREATHING RELAXATION SKILL 1

Before beginning the meditation, you may like to relax with a couple of simple shoulder and tummy breaths.

So first, just raise your shoulders towards your jaw, and hold them there for a moment, and then let them down again. Now repeat once more, only this time consciously, but naturally breathe in as you lift your shoulders, holding the breath a moment and then exhaling easily like a sigh, as you let your shoulders drop. Repeat one more time, and let yourself become aware of where and how you are, as you come to this reflection.

Re-read the Scripture text, and perhaps take a listening moment with it in quietness before turning to the reflective meditation.

In the grip of it –
storm, earthquake and fire...

I am the mountain.
I know the screaming
of the wind.
Its force stretching me
almost to breaking point.
And I hold this knowledge as prayer...

Torn away, taken by storm,
swept out of sight.
I am aware
of the earthquake
I hold this awareness
as desperate prayer...

The once level plain of my horizon
and the once even ground at my feet
dip and spin
and I am submerged into this vortex of pure experience...

Tossed sideways
losing my grip...
(But not entirely)
Because now I am stretching, grasping...
Reaching out for anyone, anything...
But
though I feel like I am tumbling
with the stones,
crying softly
against the battering wind
though I bend under it,
I am not broken...

Irretrievably.

You know the rocks
that have left the scars...
Others that have jarred and scraped
and left me scrabbling,
but not lifeless.
In the sudden silence
a silence
that
becomes
an expanding stillness.
And
into this,
I sense
a breathing space.
I breathe...

The storm is spent for now
and into the silence
barely a whisper

an inner voice
'Listen!'…
It is a whisper
calm…
Calmer…
just a whisper
repeated…

A word?
What word?…

A presence.
A calming word as presence…

Yes
I can stay with this…

Now take a moment or two to gather any insight or word you would want to take away from this time. Sense how you are feeling, body, mind and spirit, and sense how you go on from here into today or tonight… Go well.

Chapter 12

YOU, LORD,
ARE MY SHEPHERD

The Lord is my shepherd, I shall not want
He makes me lie down in green pastures;
he leads me beside still waters;
he restores my soul.
He leads me in right paths
for his name's sake.

Even though I walk through the darkest valley,
I fear no evil;
for you are with me;
your rod and your staff –
they comfort me.

You prepare a table before me
in the presence of my enemies
you anoint my head with oil;
my cup overflows.

Surely goodness and mercy shall follow me
all the days of my life,
and I shall dwell in the house of the Lord
my whole life long.

Ps 23 NRSV

SHORT BREATHING RELAXATION SKILL 2

Before beginning the meditation here is a second deep breath exercise you may wish to try. Lifting your shoulders, bring them inward and upward towards your ears, and hold them there for a moment, aware of the stretch and the warmth that goes with it, as you let the shoulders back down. Repeat this a second and third time, and then, bending your elbows, move your shoulder blades together, and gently 'wing' your elbows in and out, together and then separately, to soften and relax the muscles of your back. Now return your arms and hands to your lap, and just breathe out as though sighing. Now, for a count of four, inhale through your nose, aware of how your lower ribcage expands outwards, and then the mid-chest, and upper chest. Give a final little 'sniff' inwards before gently exhaling again through your mouth for a count of six, (or eight if you can do this easily). Don't force anything. Repeat this whole deep breath just once more, and then resume your ordinary breathing.

Now slowly read the Scripture text again and see where it takes you....

**The Lord is my Shepherd,
I shall not want.**

I reflect on these words –
I shall not want...
Is this the same as everything I want?...
What do I need?...
Thank you for what I have...

**He makes me lie down in green pastures;
he leads me beside still waters;**

I think of the moment you give me to be quiet...
When rest is important and bed or grass feels good.
I think of special meals and relaxation...

Remembering these...
Thank you...

He restores my soul.
He leads me in right paths for his name's sake.

For those who have sat with me in sickness
and operations....
Thank you.
And thank you for patience with me
when I feel weak...
Somehow you help me keep patient with myself.
And thank you
when you help me to overcome embarrassment and
respond to care
graciously
gracefully
gratefully...
Thank you...

Even though I walk through the darkest valley
I fear no evil; for you are with me;
Your rod and your staff – they comfort me.

I bring to mind the moments that have
brought me face to face with death.
Sorrow...
Danger...
Inner death...
I remember...
Thank you...

You prepare a table before me
in the presence of my enemies:

Once again,
I do have everything I need, and also all the extras,
that come as your gift.
Thank you...

You anoint my head with oil:
my cup overflows

I breathe in your blessings.
Cool air breathed in
warm air breathed out.
Naming them...
Thank you...

Surely goodness and mercy shall follow me
All the days of my life.

Thank you
I breathe in
I breathe out,
in your presence...

and I shall dwell in the house of the Lord
my whole life long.

Thank you...
Amen –
So be it...

Now take a moment or two to gather any insight or word you would
want to take away from this time. Sense how you are feeling, body
mind and spirit, and sense how you go on from here into today or
tonight... Go well.

Chapter 13

LOSS

After the death of Abram's father,
God told him, 'Leave your own country behind you,
and your own people, and go to the land I will guide
you to.'

GEN 12:1-2 LB

SHORT BREATHING RELAXATION SKILL 1

Before beginning the meditation, you may like to relax with a couple
of simple shoulder and tummy breaths.

So first, just raise your shoulders towards your jaw, and hold them
there for a moment, and then let them down again. Now repeat once
more, only this time consciously, but naturally breathe in as you lift
your shoulders, holding the breath a moment and then exhaling easily
like a sigh, as you let your shoulders drop. Repeat one more time, and
let yourself become aware of where and how you are, as you come to
this reflection.

Re-read the Scripture text, and perhaps take a listening moment
with it in quietness before turning to the reflective meditation.

'It will never be the same again',
this is what death has taught you.

You know the numbness of the early days
endless days
the loss of focus
and train of thought...
The short fuse
and sharply sudden tears
You know these...
And more...

You sense it couldn't be any other way.
Couldn't just be business as usual
You tried...
No one knows
except those who know
from experience.

That they are there
at times
allows you
at times
to talk...

And with them
or alone
the time comes
to sift through
memories
again and again
until you find goodbye
is true...

You know it will never be the same...
You face now

living with difference.
You can only sit with this
through it...

Can memory become incorporation
rather than amputation?...
You pray with this...

Impossibly faint you hear
the words 'the land I will show you...'
It will have to be so
You do not know this way alone.
But you need only to move one step
and then another...

You are ready to be shown
if not now, then some day,
the right day.

As there is life after loss
so you also live.
Yes, you can live
differently...

Now take a moment or two to gather any insight or word you would
want to take away from this time. Sense how you are feeling, body,
mind and spirit, and sense how you go on from here into today or
tonight... Go well.

Chapter 14

WRESTLING WITH
THE ANGEL

That same night he got up and crossed the ford of the Jabbock. After he had taken his (family) across the stream, he sent all his possessions over too. And Jacob was left alone. Then someone wrestled with him until daybreak, who seeing he could master him, struck him on the hip-socket, and Jacob's hip was dislocated as he wrestled with him. He said, 'let me go, for day is breaking!' Jacob replied, 'I will not let you go unless you bless me'. The other said, 'What is your name?' 'Jacob' he replied. He said, 'No longer are you to be called Jacob, but Israel since you have shown your strength against God and men and have prevailed'. Then Jacob replied, 'Please tell me your name.' He replied, 'Why do you ask my name?' With that he blessed him there. Jacob named the place Peniel, 'Because I have seen God face to face', he said, 'and survived'. The sun rose as he passed Peniel, limping because of his hip.

GEN 32: 24-32 NJB

SHORT BREATHING RELAXATION SKILL 2

Before beginning the meditation here is a second deep breath exercise you may wish to try. Lifting your shoulders, bring them inward and upward towards your ears, and hold them there for a moment, aware of the stretch and the warmth that goes with it, as you let the shoulders back down. Repeat this a second and third time, and then, bending your elbows, move your shoulder blades together, and gently 'wing' your elbows in and out, together and then separately, to soften and relax the muscles of your back. Now return your arms and hands to your lap, and just breathe out as though sighing. Now, for a count of four, inhale through your nose, aware of how your lower ribcage expands outwards, and then the mid-chest, and upper chest. Give a final little 'sniff' inwards before gently exhaling again through your mouth for a count of six, (or eight if you can do this easily). Don't force anything. Repeat this whole deep breath just once more, and then resume your ordinary breathing.

Now slowly read the Scripture text again and see where it takes you...

In your imagination, you see
in the evening dusk,
the family crossing back and forth, back and forth...
As
Jacob brings them across the river,
with all his belongings,
all he calls his own,
trying to find the best way to make peace with his brother...

But now
for some reason
he has crossed back
to be alone for a time
in solitude...

Looking at him, you realise
that you
also
come for quiet time…
From family…
And frictions…
And fighting…
Personal time for solitude…

And then you see the Other
and hear the voices
as Jacob struggles
and wrestles
with what has been false…

False in his relationships –
Brother, mother, sister, family…
False in work…
False in name…
And then,
though it
wounds him,
he is able to move
on…

Hear his true name…
Ask a blessing…

And now, that Other
turns aside to you,
with compassion.
Asking gently now,
what do *you* wrestle with
In these quiet hours?…

What will *you* not let go of
that holds you so strongly...

And you reply...
Slowly...
To this.

And perhaps it feels like wrestling
as the words and thoughts
Struggle...
Squeeze...
Hold out...
To utterance...
In greater simplicity...

And there is peace in this
like a quiet dawn
and a final question...

'*Will you bless me?*'...

*Now take a moment or two to gather any insight or word you would
want to take away from this time. Sense how you are feeling, body
mind and spirit, and sense how you go on from here into today or
tonight... Go well.*

Chapter 15

TURNING ASIDE TO HEAR

Moses was keeping the flock of his father-in-law Jethro...; he led his flock beyond the wilderness, and came to Horeb, the mountain of God.

There the angel of the Lord appeared to him in a flame of fire out of a bush; he looked, and the bush was blazing, yet it was not consumed.

Then Moses said, 'I must turn aside and look at this great sight, and see why the bush is not burned up'.

When the Lord saw that he had turned aside to see, God called to him out of the bush, 'Moses, Moses!' And he said, 'Here I am'.

Then he said, 'Come no closer! Remove the sandals from your feet, for the place on which you are standing is holy ground'. He said further, 'I am the God of your father, the God of Abraham, the God of Isaac, and the God of Jacob'.

EX 3:1-6A NRSV

SHORT BREATHING RELAXATION SKILL 1

Before beginning the meditation, you may like to relax with a couple of simple shoulder and tummy breaths.

So first, just raise your shoulders towards your jaw, and hold them there for a moment, and then let them down again. Now repeat once more, only this time consciously, but naturally breathe in as you lift your shoulders, holding the breath a moment and then exhaling easily like a sigh, as you let your shoulders drop. Repeat one more time, and let yourself become aware of where and how you are, as you come to this reflection.

Re-read the Scripture text, and perhaps take a listening moment with it in quietness before turning to the reflective meditation.

You become aware of Moses,
as your imagination allows him to be,
walking ahead, observant,
with the minding of the family flock...
And you reflect on what you also
are minding, keeping...
Family, or community...
The domestic details and all that this entails...
And you bring one aspect to prayer...

Your imagination fills with the Scripture scene –
the animals slowly mouthing the sparse green
searched out in the place beyond the desert,
with small bushes, stones,
and Mount Horeb, the 'mountain of God,' just ahead...
You see the flock wanting to perhaps settle, content to just
nibble here and there
with Moses, ahead, bringing them beyond their first choices...

And you reflect on what leads you
onward, to choose your own Mount Horeb...

A place of quiet, a place of silence
You reflect on what, if anything, holds you back from going
there...
And when it is
that you come to it...

And now it is as if you have become one with this scene
as one of the further bushes over to the side, seems to flicker
and then bursts into flames...
An ordinary bush
whoever thought a bush special?...
An ordinary bush
experienced differently...

And you reflect
on those incidents in your life
where noticing the
special in the ordinary
has shown you its Angel
– its message of insight...

There is a pause in the movement of the flock.
Moses stops. And you hear his words, *'I will turn aside...'*
You accompany him
as he goes to see,
and hear the messenger,
the *Angelos*...

Because you also approach, alongside
you are able to hear your own name being called...
Twice...

And you ask; 'Am I able to "turn aside"
from my routine...
From my preoccupations?'...

And you ask
'What at the present time in my life,
is inviting me to "turn aside" to see and turn aside to hear?...
Again'...

And as you hear Moses being requested 'Take off your shoes'
you wonder what, if anything,
stands between you
and hearing...
What urges you to be aware
that you also
stand
on Holy Ground?...

What comes between?
Your heart knows what 'removing shoes' entails
And you bring this to prayer...
To the One
who tells you
that this moment
is
Holy
Ground...

Content to be here...

*Now take a moment or two to gather any insight or word you would
want to take away from this time. Sense how you are feeling, body
mind and spirit, and sense how you go on from here into today or
tonight... Go well.*

Chapter 16

SUSTAINED

In the morning, when a layer of dew lifted,
there on the surface of the wilderness was a fine
*   flaky substance,*
as fine as frost on the ground.
When the Israelites saw it,
they said to one another,
'What is it?'...
For they did not know what it was.
Moses said to them, 'It is the bread that the Lord has
*   given you to eat.*

Ex 16:13-15 LB

SHORT BREATHING RELAXATION SKILL 2

Before beginning the meditation here is a second deep breath exercise you may wish to try. Lifting your shoulders, bring them inward and upward towards your ears, and hold them there for a moment, aware of the stretch and the warmth that goes with it, as you let the shoulders back down. Repeat this a second and third time, and then, bending your elbows, move your shoulder blades together, and gently 'wing' your elbows in and out, together and then separately, to soften and relax the muscles of your back. Now return your arms and hands to your lap, and just breathe out as though sighing. Now, for a count of four, inhale through your nose, aware of how your lower ribcage expands outwards, and then the mid-chest, and upper chest. Give a final little 'sniff' inwards before gently exhaling again through your mouth for a count of six, (or eight if you can do this easily). Don't force anything. Repeat this whole deep breath just once more, and then resume your ordinary breathing.

Now slowly read the Scripture text again and see where it takes you....

It is morning
and you see the dew
lifting...
And as you step
into the gift of an early hour
before it is fully day
perhaps you also ask the question;
'What is it?'
that is being given here
as 'manna'
for you,
too?...

You recognise a need for 'manna'
in your body and physical needs because...

And particularly...
Pray with this....

You recognise a need for manna
in your mind and thoughts because...
And particularly...
Pray with this...

You recognise a need for manna
in your feelings and emotional life because...
And particularly...
Pray with this...

You recognise a need for manna
in your spirit and prayer-life because...
And particularly...
Pray with this...

You recognise a need for manna
in your family/community life because...
And particularly...
Pray with this...

The way you are able to gather in this manna
for body is by...
For mind is by...
For emotions is by...
For spirit is by...
For family/community is by...

Each moment
is
that dawn....

Now take a moment or two to gather any insight or word you would want to take away from this time. Sense how you are feeling, body mind and spirit, and sense how you go on from here into today or tonight... Go well.

Chapter 17

DISCERNING THE WAY

'O God, My God!'
How I search for you.
How I thirst for you!
in this parched and weary land,
where there is no water,
how I long to find you.
How I wish I could go
into your sanctuary
to see your strength and glory;
for your love and kindness are better to me than life
itself.
How I praise you! I will bless you as long as I live,
Lifting up my hands to you in prayer.
At last I shall be satisfied;
I shall praise you with great joy.'

Ps 63:1-5 LB

Short Breathing Relaxation Skill 1

Before beginning the meditation, you may like to relax with a couple of simple shoulder and tummy breaths.

So first, just raise your shoulders towards your jaw, and hold them there for a moment, and then let them down again. Now repeat once more, only this time consciously, but naturally breathe in as you lift your shoulders, holding the breath a moment and then exhaling easily like a sigh, as you let your shoulders drop. Repeat one more time, and let yourself become aware of where and how you are, as you come to this reflection.

Re-read the Scripture text, and perhaps take a listening moment with it in quietness before turning to the reflective meditation.

You are the Way, the Truth and the Life.
And I am ready to search…
It's time… finally –
kairos time
time to go beyond the words

Can my yearning risk the search?…
What *do* I seek when I speak of longing?…
Perhaps the answer is in
the deeper current
subtly urging me…
While my safe self struggles.

Asking 'How exactly ?'…
While also realising that
there is no 'exactly'…

I want to go where you lead me
beyond the dryness where I find no life
and I consent

to search...
And if it means major changes,
I come back to the first sentence.

And I let myself remember
what I would miss
most....
Even as I also admit
some aspects 'Weariness without water'
would be a relief to leave

Search for you, for Life,
yes, I am filled with hope
I look forward to...

And continue to pray...

Now take a moment or two to gather any insight or word you would want to take away from this time. Sense how you are feeling, body mind and spirit, and sense how you go on from here into today or tonight... Go well.

Chapter 18

SUSTAINING EARTH

You have seen... how I brought you to myself as though on eagle's wings. Now if you will obey me, and keep your part of my contract with you, you shall be my own little flock from among all the nations of the earth; for all the earth is mine.

Ex 19:4 LB

SHORT BREATHING RELAXATION SKILL 2

Before beginning the meditation here is a second deep breath exercise you may wish to try. Lifting your shoulders, bring them inward and upward towards your ears, and hold them there for a moment, aware of the stretch and the warmth that goes with it, as you let the shoulders back down. Repeat this a second and third time, and then, bending your elbows, move your shoulder blades together, and gently 'wing' your elbows in and out, together and then separately, to soften and relax the muscles of your back. Now return your arms and hands to your lap, and just breathe out as though sighing. Now, for a count of four, inhale through your nose, aware of how your lower ribcage expands outwards, and then the mid-chest, and upper chest. Give a final little 'sniff' inwards before gently exhaling again through your mouth for a count of six, (or eight if you can do this easily). Don't force anything. Repeat this whole deep breath just once more, and then resume your ordinary breathing.

Now slowly read the Scripture text again and see where it takes you...

Soft, safe and sustained.
Your eagle-wing carrying
warms me.
And equally warns me.
I'm grateful.
You have revealed
immancence...
When is this...?
And Transcendence
How is this...?
Also mutual contract
grounded
in Your Creation...

Have I a contract with creation?...

You eagle-carrier, soar with
a vantaged vision,
unblinking responsibility.
Your eagle-wing carrying has
revealed perspective
showing
the vulnerability of earth...

How are you telling me?...

Your eagle-wing carrying
appeals to
my obedience,

grounded
in my nature
because being carried,
gathered and gathering
means
balancing commitment
with others, with yours,
as mutual sustainers
of our earth...

How can I respond to this?...

Now take a moment or two to gather any insight or word you would want to take away from this time. Sense how you are feeling, body mind and spirit, and sense how you go on from here into today or tonight... Go well.

Chapter 19

SURRENDER INTO SOLITUDE

I was helpless in the hand of God, and when he said to me, 'Go out into the valley and I will talk to you there'. I arose and went, and oh, I saw the glory of the Lord there, just as in my first vision.

EZEK 3:22-23A LB

SHORT BREATHING RELAXATION SKILL 1

Before beginning the meditation, you may like to relax with a couple of simple shoulder and tummy breaths.

So first, just raise your shoulders towards your jaw, and hold them there for a moment, and then let them down again. Now repeat once more, only this time consciously, but naturally breathe in as you lift your shoulders, holding the breath a moment and then exhaling easily like a sigh, as you let your shoulders drop. Repeat one more time, and let yourself become aware of where and how you are, as you come to this reflection.

Re-read the Scripture text, and perhaps take a listening moment with it in quietness before turning to the reflective meditation.

I was helpless in the hand of God...,

Surrender feels like inevitability.
And surrender here is positive...

I feel the inevitability of my 'yes'
drawn deeply from
a secret helplessness
which understands -
'So, of course, it's yes'...
What else can I do?...

and when he said to me, 'Go out into the valley and I will talk to you there,'...

This is not the first 'yes'...
I know where it began...
When it began...
When I saw the valley as loneliness
they have all gone on,
or I had gone on,
and it was lonely
until you spoke...

I arose and went, and oh...

I recall the words – as I heard them...
And I did go into the valley...
Climbing down
and strangely
in my helplessness
there was light and there was a change

What happened?...
Many valleys
and you spoke...

What happened?...

The valley, no longer empty dark, nor even boring grey.
Going on alone became different from lonely darkness
separate.
Because
the valley became
something in itself
solitude...

Solitude,
sometimes clearing
into a wonderful dawn.
When the morning light
folds the shadow back
and oh...

**I saw the glory of the Lord there,
just as in my first vision.**

And that is why I say 'yes'
valley solitude
feels like love.
It is love...

*Now take a moment or two to gather any insight or word you would
want to take away from this time. Sense how you are feeling, body
mind and spirit, and sense how you go on from here into today or
tonight... Go well.*

Chapter 20

SEEN OR UNSEEN

*See, I am sending my Angel before you to lead you
safely to the land I have prepared for you. Reverence
him and obey all his instructions; do not rebel
against him, for he will not pardon your
transgression; he is my representative – he bears my
name. But if you are careful to obey him, following
all my instructions, then I will be an enemy to your
enemies. For my Angel shall go before you...*

Ex 2: 20-23 LB

SHORT BREATHING RELAXATION SKILL 2

*Before beginning the meditation here is a second deep breath exercise
you may wish to try. Lifting your shoulders, bring them inward and
upward towards your ears, and hold them there for a moment, aware
of the stretch and the warmth that goes with it, as you let the
shoulders back down. Repeat this a second and third time, and then,
bending your elbows, move your shoulder blades together, and gently
'wing' your elbows in and out, together and then separately, to soften
and relax the muscles of your back. Now return your arms and hands
to your lap, and just breathe out as though sighing. Now, for a count*

of four, inhale through your nose, aware of how your lower ribcage expands outwards, and then the mid-chest, and upper chest. Give a final little 'sniff' inwards before gently exhaling again through your mouth for a count of six, (or eight if you can do this easily). Don't force anything. Repeat this whole deep breath just once more, and then resume your ordinary breathing.

Now slowly read the Scripture text again and see where it takes you....

Is it day or is it night?
And what exactly am I looking for? Or at?...
If I knew whether it was day
or night
I might recognise your presence more easily...

What does a cloud by day or fire by night really look like?...

It is what is most distinguishable.
Cloud is not easily seen at night, and fire is lost by day.

Who needs a cloud's shade at night?...
Or the bright warmth of fire in daytime?...
So what do I see today
which
is both distinguishable
and useful?...
Can that be your way of sending the Angel?...

Now take a moment or two to gather any insight or word you would want to take away from this time. Sense how you are feeling, body mind and spirit, and sense how you go on from here into today or tonight... Go well.

Chapter 21

NEW SKIN...
HEALTHY BONES

.... 'Can these bones come to life?'
'Lord God' I answered, 'you alone know that.'
Then he said to me, 'Prophesy over these bones, and
say to them, 'dry bones, hear the word of the Lord.'
Thus says the Lord God to these bones: 'See! I will
bring spirit into you, that you may come to life.'

EZEK 37:1-5 NAB

SHORT BREATHING RELAXATION SKILL 1

Before beginning the meditation, you may like to relax with a couple
of simple shoulder and tummy breaths.

So first, just raise your shoulders towards your jaw, and hold them
there for a moment, and then let them down again. Now repeat once
more, only this time consciously, but naturally breathe in as you lift
your shoulders, holding the breath a moment and then exhaling easily
like a sigh, as you let your shoulders drop. Repeat one more time, and
let yourself become aware of where and how you are, as you come to
this reflection.

Re-read the Scripture text, and perhaps take a listening moment
with it in quietness before turning to the reflective meditation.

Lying here,
with all that surrounds you,
sight and sound and sensitivities,
you seem to hear, as if from afar, the words,
'Prophesy over these bones'
and you hear them, these strange words,
as applying to you...
Here, now.
So you rest back against your cushions,
or pillow
and perhaps your bones
feel heavy
in their weakness...
Any movement shrunk
by anticipation
of the effort...

It seems all you can do
the best you can do,
is just be where you are
presence to Presence
proving nothing to anyone,
but learning to be earth –
quiet dew-receiving earth,
tiny sips of living
This moment...
The next moment...
Silent reception...

The prophecy
promises Spirit
Spirit transforming frustration...
Spirit transforming impatience...
Spirit transforming regrets...

Spirit transforming suffering...
Spirit transforming pain...

'I will bring Spirit to you'
you do not have to do it.
Only lie here
And hearing the promise,
offer these bones...
gathering the spirit to your
own centre

Receive....
Breath on breath
Life-giving...

Now take a moment or two to gather any insight or word you would want to take away from this time. Sense how you are feeling, body mind and spirit, and sense how you go on from here into today or tonight... Go well.

Chapter 22

AT LAST!

I will give thanks to you, O Lord,
With all my heart,
(for you have heard the words of my mouth)
in the presence of the angels I will
sing your praise;
I will worship at your holy temple
And give thanks to your name,
Because of your kindness and truth;
For you have made great above all things
Your name and your promise.
 When I called, you answered me;
You built up strength within me...

Ps 138: 1-4 NAB

Short Breathing Relaxation Skill 2

Before beginning the meditation here is a second deep breath exercise you may wish to try. Lifting your shoulders, bring them inward and upward towards your ears, and hold them there for a moment, aware of the stretch and the warmth that goes with it, as you let the shoulders back down. Repeat this a second and third time, and then, bending your elbows, move your shoulder blades together, and gently 'wing' your elbows in and out, together and then separately, to soften and relax the muscles of your back. Now return your arms and hands to your lap, and just breathe out as though sighing. Now, for a count of four, inhale through your nose, aware of how your lower ribcage expands outwards, and then the mid-chest, and upper chest. Give a final little 'sniff' inwards before gently exhaling again through your mouth for a count of six, (or eight if you can do this easily). Don't force anything. Repeat this whole deep breath just once more, and then resume your ordinary breathing.

Now slowly read the Scripture text again and see where it takes you....

It's happened –
you have waited, and tried, and hoped and struggled
and now you're there
you acknowledge the feeling that tells you why it is so good to
have finally arrived, achieved, received...

You let your heartbeat bring you into your heart space
as you find the feelings of that centre
expanding to include your whole body...

You hold the reality of what is so good right now
and live the experience in thanksgiving...

Allowing wonder to bubble up...
Allowing gratefulness...

Allowing relief...
Allowing words
allow your heart and body and spirit to be here
bathing in praise and thanks and gratitude...
Just in the now...
With this Giver
of all this...

Stay here...

Now take a moment or two to gather any insight or word you would want to take away from this time. Sense how you are feeling, body mind and spirit, and sense how you go on from here into today or tonight... Go well.

Chapter 23

EVERYTHING IN ITS OWN TIME

A time for giving birth,
A time for dying;
A time for planting,
A time for uprooting what has been planted.
A time for killing,
A time for healing;
A time for knocking down,
A time for building.
A time for tears,
A time for laughter;
A time for mourning,
A time for dancing.
A time for throwing stones away,
A time for gathering them;
A time for embracing,
A time to refrain from embracing.
A time for searching,
A time for losing.
A time for keeping
A time for discarding.
A time for tearing,
A time for sewing;

A time for keeping silent,
A time for speaking.
A time for loving,
A time for hating;
A time for war,
A time for peace.

ECCL 3:1-8 NJB

SHORT BREATHING RELAXATION SKILL 1

Before beginning the meditation, you may like to relax with a couple of simple shoulder and tummy breaths.

So first, just raise your shoulders towards your jaw, and hold them there for a moment, and then let them down again. Now repeat once more, only this time consciously, but naturally breathe in as you lift your shoulders, holding the breath a moment and then exhaling easily like a sigh, as you let your shoulders drop. Repeat one more time, and let yourself become aware of where and how you are, as you come to this reflection.

Re-read the Scripture text, and perhaps take a listening moment with it in quietness before turning to the reflective meditation.

I choose the phrase that makes me nod my head.
Yes, this is what I find is happening.
It seems it is a 'time to ....'
I repeat the phrase in my heart,
only this time I insert the words
'for me' immediately after
'A time ....
It is a time for me to...
And I feel it in my heart...
And I invite the feelings
to take space....

Each different feeling
giving it 'time' too
time to reveal its location...
Time to show its
size and shape...

Time to change shape,
time to find words,
time to allow prayer

And then if it feels right,
I re-read the whole passage again
and this time I notice
the other verbs...
And
note as I pass, that I have also
lived some of these...

I sit with this
as with an image of the
history
of life as I have lived it...
And with whom I've lived it...
These words
denoting whole experiences...
Held, but not held onto –

I stay with the Word
that fits my prayer today...

*Now take a moment or two to gather any insight or word you would
want to take away from this time. Sense how you are feeling, body
mind and spirit, and sense how you go on from here into today or
tonight... Go well.*

Chapter 24

THE RETURN
OF THE DOVE

At the end of forty days Noah opened the window he had made in the ark and released a raven, which flew back and forth as it waited for the waters to dry up the earth. He then released a dove, to see whether the waters were receding from the surface of the earth. But the dove, finding nowhere to perch, returned to him in the ark, for there was water over the whole surface of the earth; putting out his hand he took hold of it and brought it back into the ark with him. After waiting seven more days he again released the dove from the ark. In the evening the dove came back to him, and there in its beak was a freshly picked olive-leaf. After waiting seven more days, he released the dove, and now it returned to him no more.

GEN 8:6-12 NJB

Short Breathing Relaxation Skill 2

Before beginning the meditation here is a second deep breath exercise you may wish to try. Lifting your shoulders, bring them inward and upward towards your ears, and hold them there for a moment, aware of the stretch and the warmth that goes with it, as you let the shoulders back down. Repeat this a second and third time, and then, bending your elbows, move your shoulder blades together, and gently 'wing' your elbows in and out, together and then separately, to soften and relax the muscles of your back. Now return your arms and hands to your lap, and just breathe out as though sighing. Now, for a count of four, inhale through your nose, aware of how your lower ribcage expands outwards, and then the mid-chest, and upper chest. Give a final little 'sniff' inwards before gently exhaling again through your mouth for a count of six, (or eight if you can do this easily). Don't force anything. Repeat this whole deep breath just once more, and then resume your ordinary breathing.

Now slowly read the Scripture text again and see where it takes you....

In your imagination
as if from far above,
you can see the ark...
Dipping, rising to the swell and ebb of the water...
Dark water, incomprehensible water
Water that doesn't belong here.

Descending nearer, you notice
the tiny windows just free of the swell,
but spattered when the waves spit upwards...
You identify with them
spattered as you can feel
as you can be...

You watch as the protective shutters
of one of these windows

opens just enough for
a small black raven to be released...
A searcher for help,
a way out, a way through.
You watch it slowly zigzag back and forth,
darting here and there...
Over the waters, glad to be out of it, but unable to help.
You identify with that...
Like the raven you have also made efforts to
find land
the land of reconciliation...
In the ebb and tide of relationships...
Efforts which have also found you
battling currents and spray

You watch as the raven's efforts bring it
all the same back to the ark,
and it is drawn down inside once more.
You identify with that...
All the effort, all the time
and for what?...

You bring your gaze back to the ark
and now, in your imagination,
you are nearer still...
In fact you are standing at that little window,
open again,
and Noah is beside you...
He reaches into the folds of a cloak
and passes you a small, warmly-feathered dove...
It rests trustingly in your palm,
and you feel the tiny beat of its heart
fragile, but rhythmic...

You feel yourself encouraged to place the dove
on the window's edge

– the waters still moving uncertainly below you.
It perches there, alert,
surveying all round,
missing nothing,
but not yet ready to move.

You reflect on your own ability
to also watch and wait, alert for a signal...
And it comes here! With a gentle nudge to the tail feathers,
the one beside you urges the dove upward,
and you both watch it circle and circle again
before trying one particular direction.
Your hope rises, but like the raven
the dove is forced to return.
You identify with that...
Is it still worth trying yet another time?...

Wisdom answers you
and
once more you stand with Noah,
at the window of hope...
And this time, as the dove rises in a new wind
it is almost as if you have joined it up there,
Your movements guided and supported on new thermal
currents...
And as you look down
the waters just seem
a little less threatening,
and less all-encompassing...
Enough still,
but from where you are now,
some distance from the ark
you see the mound and stubble of high ground appearing
like the first emergence from birth
altruistic space...

And a place perhaps of re-building
from what has survived.
Always something from common ground.
And the dove holds a symbol in its beak.

You know that for you then
it will be more than a symbol
it will be reality.
Perhaps you can also choose a leaf
holding it with wisdom
within the ark,
knowing that this can be a new beginning
the flood is receding
you have seen the dove...

Pray with this...

Now take a moment or two to gather any insight or word you would want to take away from this time. Sense how you are feeling, body mind and spirit, and sense how you go on from here into today or tonight... Go well.